The
HEART
of
HELPS

TAKING YOUR PLACE

by

Tom Rutherford

Unless otherwise indicated, all Scripture quotations are taken from the *King James Version* of the Bible.

The Scripture quotation marked MSG is taken from *The Message*. Copyright © 1993, 2002, 2018 by Eugene H. Peterson.

The Scripture quotation marked AMP is taken from *The Amplified Bible, Old Testament.* Copyright © 2015 by The Lockman Foundation, La Habra, CA 90631. All rights reserved.

All Scripture quotations marked TPT are taken from *The Passion Translation.*® Copyright © 2017 by BroadStreet Publishing® Group, LLC. Used by permission. All rights reserved. thePassionTranslation.com

The Heart of Helps — Taking Your Place
ISBN: 978-1-949106-44-2
Copyright © 2020 by
Tom Rutherford
P. O. Box 120081
Melbourne, Florida 32912 U.S.A.

Word & Spirit Publishing
P.O. Box 701403
Tulsa, OK 74170

Cover/Text Design: Lisa Simpson
SimpsonProductions.net

Printed in the United States of America. All rights reserved under International Copyright Law. Contents and/or cover may not be reproduced in whole or in part in any form without the express written consent of the Publisher.

Contents

Dedication 5

Foreword 7

Introduction 9

A Prayer for You 12

1 What Is the Ministry of Helps? 13

2 The Visual of the Ministry of Helps 23

3 Finding Your Place in the
   Body of Christ 31

4 Called, Appointed, and Anointed
   for Ministry of Helps 41

5 Faithfulness in Serving 55

6 Joy and Peace in Serving 75

7 Seeing the Grand Scheme
   While Serving 85

About the Author 90

Special Acknowledgement

Kathy and I want to add a special thanks to Lisa Simpson and Marilyn Price for their input and part in making this happen.

DEDICATION

In 1976, meeting Buddy, as he was lovingly referred to by both family and friends, I saw something I knew God wanted to impart to me. Kathy and my relationship grew with both Buddy and Pat Harrison to include working with both the church organization and the publishing house for over twenty years. We still maintain our relationship with Mrs. Harrison and the FCF organization.

Buddy and Pat were founders of Faith Christian Fellowship International. He served as President of the organization from 1977 until he went home to be with the Lord on November 28, 1998. The Lord instructed Buddy to be a Pastor to Pastors and Ministers, providing guidance which included the Ministry of Helps for them to succeed in the spiritual and natural realms.

The Heart of Helps

As the founder and chairman of Harrison House Publishers, Buddy obeyed God's vision to provide ministers a vehicle by which to put their message in print. Buddy successfully incorporated his knowledge and skills of the corporate world with the Lord's calling on his life. Most of what I share in this book came as a result of digesting what was taught from these two wonderful people who, one day while ministering in Michigan, heard God say, "Go back to Tulsa and start a family church, a charismatic teaching center, and reach the world."

I want to thank them for their obedience which helped many young ministers and some not so young over the years to become the gift to the Body of Christ to help build God's Kingdom and reach the world.

Foreword

I have been able to minister in over 3,000 churches and have my teachings in over 30,000 Bible Schools on the Ministry of Helps over these last 40 years. It is refreshing to see others taking up the mantle of Helps. Tom Rutherford brings a refreshing insight into the Ministry of Helps. Having known Tom for over 30 years and watching his life in ministry this book reveals the heart of a true servant. I was told many years ago that there are two attitudes in serving, the Have to and Want to. This book helps to create the Want To in the Local Church and it will be a great addition to everyone's library.

A Pastor's Friend,
Dr. Buddy Bell
www.mohi.org

INTRODUCTION

Over the years I have watched and worked with many ministries who had an emphasis on the Ministry of Helps. In the late 70s, one of the ministries which came to the forefront of the church was that of Buddy Harrison. He was even referred to as the Apostle of Helps. He imparted his insight and helped many men and women develop this gift of Helps found in 1 Corinthians 12:28, which is listed along with the other gifts for the Body of Christ.

During a period, he had a School of Helps in Tulsa at the church. Some of the people from the school began traveling to do "Helps Seminars" in churches nationally and internationally to help develop Ministry of Helps in the local churches and ministries.

Many of these young ministers went on to answer the call to walk in the offices other than Helps, but would always say along with Buddy, "I will always be in the Ministry of Helps."

The Ministry of Helps are individuals of resource and courage in the church or ministry helping the Ministry Gifts.

From this book I hope to inspire those who read it to acquire a greater knowledge of the Ministry of Helps and the importance of the calling for the end-time Church so you will become *"skilled servant workers, working from the heart within the Body of Christ, moving in rhythm and at ease with each other, efficient and graceful with each other, fully developed within and without."*

While I was praying one day, I heard the Spirit of God say, *"Great will be those*

Introduction

helping to reveal the Spirit in the end times. Not just a couple holding up the arms of the Ministry Gift, but an army led by the Spirit to help Him orchestrate the moving to manifest His glory and power. It will free the Ministry Gift to step into the glory and see and know His plan which will be grand; and many shall come to enter into the river that is flowing."

As you read the pages of this book, may it bring you to understand your call to Helps and find your place in the Body of Christ as a member in particular and receive the blessings that come because of faithfulness to serve.

A Prayer for You

Father, I thank You that those who are reading this book will receive Your plan and purpose that will change and affect their life. Faith comes by hearing and hearing by the Word of God, and the Word will come forth.

It is the Word of God that will change and affect their lives and cause great faith to come in Jesus' name.

1

WHAT IS THE MINISTRY OF HELPS?

Someone asked me, "What is the Ministry of Helps?" That is a truth in the Bible that everyone in the Body of Christ should have an understanding about. Not everyone may be called to stand behind a pulpit and preach or pastor, but we are all called to bring our part to help the work of God. There are great rewards in it. Praise God! There are great blessings in it also!

The Ministry of Helps is a calling. It begins in the spiritual realm and flows into the natural so one can function where necessary as a part of the local church or ministry. Many in the Ministry of Helps have fallen asleep, but they are beginning to wake up again! Though it may have been years, they are finding it is not too late to stir up the calling to serve. They have found they still have the same graces necessary to function in a church regardless of their age. It may have seemed that the heart to serve had an attack of A-fib (which in the natural is a form of a heart attack and may need an electrical stimulation to put it back in rhythm).

The Holy Ghost is jump-starting the servant's heart and putting it back into rhythm to function again in the Ministry of Helps. The Holy Ghost is saying to these people once again that there are no limitations, no hesitations, and no reservations in any form to hold them back. They will move in a mighty way in their place; the streams of people will come to help build the Body of Christ. They will be the members that supply with passion what is needed in this hour.

The purpose of this book is to help you to realize how necessary the Ministry of Helps is for the Body of Christ. The Armorbearer will help reveal in the services the excellence of the moving of the Holy Spirit and the Ministry Gift as a flawless seam of thread weaving a tapestry for God. Everyone in the Body of Christ has a part in helping to bring about the manifestation of His glory!

Ephesians 4:11-14,16 states:

And he gave some, apostles; and some, prophets; and some, evangelists; and some, pastors and teachers;

For the perfecting of the saints, for the work of the ministry, for the edifying of the body of Christ:

Till we all come in the unity of the faith, and of the knowledge of the Son of God, unto a perfect man, unto the measure of the stature of the fulness of Christ:

That we henceforth be no more children, tossed to and fro, and carried about with every wind of doctrine, by the sleight of men, and cunning craftiness, whereby they lie in wait to deceive; . . .

From whom the whole body fitly joined together and compacted by that which every joint supplieth, according to the effectual working in the measure of every part, maketh increase of the body unto the edifying of itself in love.

The key phrase is "maketh increase, edifies by love of the Body or to the Body."

For what God wants to do in the local church through the fivefold Ministry Gifts, there must be members of that Body in the proper place. That supply comes from the Ministry of Helps.

Here are a couple of excellent statements about the Ministry of Helps from Dr. Buddy Bell, whose life has also been an inspiration to many (including me) as he has traveled and taught on Helps for almost forty years.

First, *"There is no hierarchy in the gifts of God; the ministry of the church does not rest on status, but service. No gift that serves others is little."*

Another statement he makes is: *"People who just fit in by love, fellowship, and prayer, and often subordinate service, fill up the innumerable places, and become countless links, and without them all else would fail."*

First Corinthians 12:28 starts out concerning spiritual gifts. It says it does not want us to be ignorant. In Ephesians 4:11 we read about the apostle, prophet, evangelist, pastor, and teacher who are Spiritual Gifts. They are given to the Church for the edifying of the Body that we might grow up into Christ in all things. Chapter 12 of 1 Corinthians is telling us that we are to come together, every joint supplying the need in the Church. We need to know what joint and what supply we are!

In verse 12 it says, *"For as the body is one, and hath many members, and all the members of that one body, being many, are one body: so also, is Christ."*

In verse 28 it says, *"And God hath set some in the church, first apostles, secondarily prophets, thirdly teachers, after that miracles, then gifts of healings, **helps**, governments, diversities of tongues."*

Most of us understand the gifts of the apostle, prophet, the teacher, the miracles, governments, and diversities of tongues. Most of us have seen these in operation, but we must get a stronger understanding of the gift of Helps also found in verse 28. It is a spiritual gift given to the Church also. It requires that people fulfill their place in the Church. Raise your hand if you are a "people." I thought so. I did not think there were any non-people reading this book! We are all people. We are all joints that supply to the Body of Christ.

I supply where I am supposed to supply; and as you add your supply, it increases the Church. I have set my heart to help people find their place in the Body to function as God has called them! I want to encourage you and stir up your heart to see that God has a better plan for you than just coming to every church service and sitting in a pew or chair. He has brought you much insight into the blessings of God. Enjoy what God has for your life by letting yourself loose to serve!

As I look at the different churches and the people involved, it seems as though they have strings attached to things that keep them from serving. I would like to take a pair of scissors and cut the strings to loose them to serve. But that is what the Word of God will do; it will act as a pair of scissors that will cut you loose to serve Him!

What Is the Ministry of Helps?

I remember in the very beginning of my ministry I asked the Lord, "Lord, I don't know what to do," and He said, "I want you to serve a certain minister." I called this person up and I said, "The Lord has told me that I am to serve you!" And he said, "I don't have that. I am not going to say it won't work, but at this point I don't know." So I went back and prayed.

At that time, an opportunity to work for a publishing house was presented to me. The Lord spoke to me, and He said, "Will you serve the leader of this organization as you would have served the other minister?" "Yes!" was my answer, and I began to serve him. I did that for twenty-three years. Did I serve the other minister? Yes, I did! I served him in many ways because he was involved with the publishing house. Did the blessings of God come? Yes! Did I get opportunities to work with him? Yes! I cannot count the number of times I had opportunities to work with both of them. I continue to count the blessings daily which came from serving these two Gifts to the Body of Christ.

2

The Visual of the Ministry of Helps

There comes a point in time where you must understand that the spiritual qualifications to serve come, and then you must keep your commitment to God. Keeping your heart right before God makes you a visible, realistic standard of servanthood in the local church. A good example of this is made more visible in 1 Kings 10:4-8:

> *And when the queen of Sheba had seen all Solomon's wisdom, and the house that he had built,*
>
> *And the meat of his table, and the sitting of his servants, and the attendance of his ministers, and their apparel, and his cupbearers, and his ascent by which he went up unto the house of the Lord; there was no more spirit in her.*
>
> *And she said to the king, It was a true report that I heard in mine own land of thy acts and of thy wisdom.*
>
> *Howbeit I believed not the words, until I came, and mine eyes had seen it: and, behold, the half was not told me: thy wisdom and prosperity exceedeth the fame which I heard.*

The Visual of the Ministry of Helps

Happy are thy men, happy are these thy servants, which stand continually before thee, and that hear thy wisdom.

Notice verse 8: "HAPPY ARE THESE THY SERVANTS!"

Much of what is going on in different parts of the Church is the unveiling of the supernatural. This new visual must stand alongside of the Ministry Gift as Sheba saw in Solomon. She did not hear Solomon's wisdom. She saw it! This can be simply stated as, "*The visual presented by a properly functioning Ministry of Helps flowing in the supernatural, naturally.*" That is why we must begin to develop and train about Helps and its value to the Church. There are men, women, and young people who need to know how important it is to be behind the scenes being faithful, and then at the right season, God brings promotion. Promotion may be to a fivefold Ministry Gift or stepping into leadership in the Ministry of Helps.

In Acts 6, starting in verse 1, seven were called and set in place to minister in Helps so the apostles could stay focused on the Word. One of the seven we hear of is Stephen preaching with signs and wonders, and then Philip the evangelist who had a greater impact on the people. But I am sure they continued to serve and help the apostles.

I want every one of you to be a visible, realistic standard of the servanthood in the local church by doing what you are supposed be doing for God!

CLARIFY, SIMPLIFY, AND PURIFY

God gave me, specifically, three words as Kathy, my wife, and I were praying. It was clarify, simplify, and purify. To me the Ministry of Helps must be clear, simple, and a matter of the (pure) heart first, and then the technical action necessary will come much more easily.

1. I want to **clarify** some things for you in this teaching, and that is to get you free from confusion and doubt. I want to make it plain and help you rid the obstructions and the entanglements of your life so that you can obey God.

2. I want to **simplify**, render serving less complex to know, that it is not hard to work in the Ministry of Helps. It is not hard to find your place and calling in the Body of Christ. It is not hard to be a joint that supplies what God wants in the Body of Christ. You can find that place, you can be that individual, and you can cause increase in a church because you are supplying your part. Amen!

3. Then He said **purify,** which means to rid ourselves of impurities, (wrong mind-sets). I want to make sure that you understand first the spiritual application and your position spiritually to what must happen in your life before you step into the Ministry of Helps.

Ministries fail every day. The apostle, prophet, evangelist, pastor, and teacher fail because they do not keep their spiritual life right. They try to live off the fruit of their calling. They need to dedicate, commit, and fill themselves up and live on the Word on a regular basis which helps keep their spiritual life right.

You cannot just walk into the Ministry of Helps and expect that because you are doing something that you are going to be okay spiritually. It does not work that way. It never will work that way. You will burn out, you will get caught up, you'll

The Visual of the Ministry of Helps

miss God, and you'll become a wandering generality. I do not want that to happen. I want to make sure that you stay right. That will happen from continuing daily in the Word, worshipping and spending time with God, and doing things that you are supposed be doing.

3

Finding Your Place in the Body of Christ

Judges 7:21 says, *"And they stood every man in his place round about the camp; and all the host ran, and cried, and fled."*

It's talking about Gideon's 300 men with their pots and their lamps, hand picked and qualified. They were there and they were narrowed down from 32,000 to

300. That is a lot of people who were let go. They got their pots and lamps, and then got into position as instructed.

If you do not hear from God, get in a place of prayer and spend time with God to find out what you're supposed to be doing in the Body of Christ. When you read this verse, it talks about every man being in a place. This helps us understand the chief purpose of the local church. The local church is to help you find your place in the Body of Christ. Then you are to train and discipline yourself to yield to that place.

I once heard someone say that discipline weighs ounces, but regret weighs tons. Do not sit around in the church and not discipline yourself to do what you know you are supposed to be doing for the Body of Christ. Regret will come and weigh you down. But when you obey, it will seem light as a feather. Discipline will bring great rewards from God! Obedience will bring great rewards from God!

What happens when everyone gets in their place in the church? Have you ever asked yourself that question? If every member in the Body was in their place in the church, what would happen? What would happen to the local church if everyone were working in the place they are supposed to be working, doing what they're supposed to be doing for God? Growth would come! But also, peace would come because things get jointly fitted together.

What happens when your own physical body gets out of whack in one area or another? It is not very peaceful, is it? You do not have peace in your life. You are in turmoil, and you are in strife with yourself. So, get in your place and experience peace in your life, the God-kind of peace. In Ephesians 4:16 it says that you, as a member in the Body of Christ, have a particular calling, just like the apostle, the prophet, the evangelist, the pastor, and the teacher.

Notice again in 1 Corinthians 12:28, it does not say singular, "Help"—it says plural "Helps." So there is more than one area of "Helps." That means every individual has a place or position. You need to find out what it is so you will be fulfilled. Do you realize that if you are not working in the Ministry of Helps and doing something in the local church, you're not being fulfilled? You are just half fulfilled! I want to be totally fulfilled!

When I was working in the Ministry of Helps, my wife and I could not wait to get to the church! We were so fulfilled in serving and doing what God had called us to do and knew that the blessings of God were abounding in our lives. Because of our faithfulness, our children were in the blessing line also. They were serving right alongside of us. We knew that God had promised us that if we would be faithful that we would have an abundance of supply in our lives, and the blessings of God would overtake us.

As we continued to work in the Ministry of Helps, we saw others getting in their place, and that brought a peace in our church. Guess what happens when peace comes on the pastor and the ministerial staff? The supernatural manifestation of God begins to happen! It becomes visual and ushers in God!

Ephesians 4:16 says, *"From whom the whole body fitly joined together and compacted by that which every joint supplieth, according to the effectual working in the measure of every part, maketh increase of the body unto the edifying of itself in love."*

We talked about in 1 Corinthians, chapter 12, that the Body is one, and the Body also is Christ. If every joint together compacted, supplies according to the effectual working measure of every part, maketh increase of the Body, what Body is he talking about? He is talking about the Body of Christ. Growth definitely comes when you're doing what you're supposed to be doing in the Body.

It says every joint effectually working together. Vine's says "effectually" means: active, powerful in action, full of power to achieve results. When you are in the right position in the Ministry of Helps, you become a group of people who are moving forward and achieving great actions for God. Your church becomes a force that is unstoppable on the face of the earth. It will not be hard to find people to do what needs to be done. If everyone is in their place, it will not be hard to reach out and touch your community, surrounding cities, and the world! It will not be hard; it would not be hard at all.

First Corinthians 12:12 says the Body has many members as we have talked about. If there are many members, there are also particulars. Find your particular place in the Body of Christ, a part of the Ministry of Helps. Get in it, do what you're supposed to, and get blessed!

I have used the phrase, "the particular place," and wanted to give you my definition: *"The worker who moves into the particular place, makes the experience of each individual much more effective. Each one becomes a real person about whom we know enough to appreciate the real experience as part of a larger operation of Kingdom work!"*

It is that simple! That is why God says to simplify it. It is not hard, it's not complex, and it's not going to be difficult for you to find your place. This causes an edifying of the whole Body.

"Edifying" means: bringing instruction or improvement; spiritually improving in morale and the knowledge to build. It brings insight along with knowledge and understanding. When you are in your place and your position in the Body of Christ, then the church gets built. It takes labor. It takes individuals doing what they are supposed to be doing for God.

The second thing that happens when each member in particular gets in their place, power comes! A demonstration of power in the church means the devil flees, souls are saved, the sick will be healed, and Christ will be lifted up! That is what you want to see in the Church today! We want to see the devil fleeing. We want to see people who are tormented set free! God is ready for every member, in particular, to be in a place and position where they supply to the Church so it can grow. It can grow in peace and in power!

First Corinthians 12:25-26 says:

That there should be no schism in the body; but that the members should have the same care one for another.

And whether one member suffer, all the members suffer with it; or one member be honoured, all the members rejoice with it.

If we are all joined together as one member and one Body, there is no schism among us, there is no division, there is no strife, there is nothing that can separate our Body. There is nothing that can come and separate the members of our Body.

4

CALLED, APPOINTED, AND ANOINTED FOR MINISTRY OF HELPS

Did God call you? Did God send you? God does not call anybody or send them anywhere unless He equips them. If you are called and sent, then you are equipped to do something in the Body. Help God fulfill what He wants in a local church and ministry so that people might be set free and delivered from the snare of the devil.

Whether you are working in the nursery, children's church, the parking lot, or wherever, know it is a valuable and precious work to God. It is not little; it is not small. There are no little things in the eyes of God when it comes to serving.

First Peter 4:10-11 says:

As every man hath received the gift, even so minister the same one to another, as good stewards of the manifold grace of God.

If any man speak, let him speak as the oracles of God; if any man minster, let him do it as of the ability which God giveth: that God in all things may be glorified through Jesus Christ, to whom be praise and dominion for ever and ever. Amen.

Verse 11 in *The Passion Translation* says,

"For example, if you have a speaking gift, speak as though God were speaking his words through you. If you have the gift of serving, do it passionately with the strength God gives you, so that in everything God alone will be glorified through Jesus Christ. For to him belong the power and the glory forever throughout all ages! Amen."

Because Christ taught us how to serve, God will not look down on His own Son and say it was little what He did. He will not look down on you and see little, small, or insignificant as you are doing your part. When you are serving in the local church, no act of serving is insignificant. All positions are powerful to God.

HAVING VISION

It brings great honor and great glory to God when everyone is in their place. When everyone is in their place, we find faithful support of the vision. Do you realize that?

When every part of my physical body is working like it should, then I have no symptoms. Nothing in my body is keeping me or hindering me from operating in the perfection in which God created it.

We want to make sure people understand the vision.

When your body does not feel well or does not fit together right, what do you usually want to do? Go rest or go to sleep. So, what happens when you go to sleep? You shut your eyes and have no vision.

We need to be awakened to the vision to help!

Smith Wigglesworth said: *"Being awakened does not particularly mean you are asleep; it means that you might be dense to activity relating to the spiritual realm. So, God is causing us to understand that we have to be alive and awakened."*

The questions I have for you are, "Are you jointly fitted together? Are you helping your church continue to see and fulfill the vision that God has for it?" If you are faithful to attend, you will find other people becoming faithful. Available, dependable, and trustworthy people begin to rise and find that God has a place for them in the local church. That is what happens. They understand that there is a spiritual perspective for what God wants for their lives. They are called, appointed, and anointed for such a time as this.

They may have recognized the call ten years ago, but they are called, appointed, and anointed for such a time as this.

First Peter 5:5 TPT says:

In the same way, the younger ones should willingly support the leadership of the elders. In every relationship, each of you must wrap around yourself the apron of a humble servant. Because: God resists you when you are proud but multiplies grace and favor when you are humble.

I am called, appointed, and anointed for such a time as this, that I might see the manifestation of the glory of God, that I might see the glory on people's faces and see it manifested in their lives. I will see it ever present everywhere I go and see what God is going to do before the return of Jesus Christ.

I am going to be in my place, I am going to be doing what I am supposed to be doing. I believe that is what I am doing right now today. I believe that I do not have to convince myself over and over. I must enforce what I am doing is what God told me to do. I am doing what I am supposed to be doing.

When you have friends who come up to you and ask, "What in the world are you volunteering down at the church for? Why are you giving all your time down there? Come on, go with me. Let's go fishing! You do not have to go to church Sunday; they won't miss you." Yes, they will! We need every joint supplying. Without you, the church is hurting! You have a supply that God has given to you.

Gideon, after narrowing down his army, gave instructions. They stood in their place, and they did not break ranks.

Follow After the Peace of God

One of the biggest stumbling blocks for us today is that we do not always choose our right place. Sometimes we get out of peace because we do not have the right to choose. You know, it goes back to me, myself, and I. I want to do what I want to do, God. I want to sing on the platform. I want to play the piano. I want to work in the nursery. Just follow peace and what your heart is saying to do.

Many in the Body of Christ need to assure themselves that their heart is in charge. It may not be necessarily what our physical body or our mind thinks is the best thing for us to do. The best thing for us to do is to obey God and to see the blessings of God come to pass in our lives.

I hear a lot of people saying, "I don't know what I want to do." My response is, "You know you should be serving and supplying because I've given you Scriptures. They show that you should be serving and supplying as a member in particular in the Body of Christ or as the joint that supplieth according to God's plan and purpose for the local church." Amen. So, you know that!

A lot of times we do not feel like we know what we should do. We feel like we need to ask somebody. Well, ask your pastor. Say, "I want to help somewhere. What can I do?" And he will get you involved! It may only be a temporary place. Then, while you are serving, you might get a specific direction in your heart; and then you will need to follow that. But if you are not doing anything, do something.

See the blessings of God come in your life when you are doing something for God. He is going to reward your faithfulness! Proverbs 25:13 says a faithful messenger will refresh the soul of his masters. He will also abound in favor.

Even if it is just passing out tracts, that is great. If you just come and warm a seat every service, it is hurting the pastor, it is hurting you, and it is hurting other people around you. It is affecting you, me, and everyone else when you are not supplying that part that you are supposed to be in the Body.

It says in Judges 7:20 that the three companies blew the trumpets and smashed the jars, grasping the torches in their left hands and holding in their right hands the trumpets they were to blow. Then they shouted, "The sword of the Lord, and of Gideon." As Gideon spoke and instructed to break the pitchers, then God turned the armies against themselves. Everybody was in their place, fitted together, linked arm to arm, holding their pots. Whatever they were doing, no ranks were broken! They obeyed the call, obeyed the directions, and obeyed what God said to do! God said what to do through Gideon, and the enemy was defeated.

That is what will happen in a local church. You follow God's instructions through the pastor and the enemy will be defeated. Leadership can help you find your place in the Body, and they are counting on you being in your place. Do not break ranks is all I can say. Find your place, be strong in His army, and respond! Be strong in the local church!

Our value is not in what we do, but in who we are. Do not get concerned about the value in what you do. People may think less of you, but it is not what you do, it is who you are. It is who you are in Christ. People will see your servant's heart, your Christlike attitude, and more of all the fruit of the Spirit working and operating in you when you get in your place, obey God, and do what you're supposed to do in the Ministry of Helps.

HELP BUILD THE WALL!

There has always been an attitude in the Church to try to keep people from doing what they are doing. In Nehemiah 6:3, Nehemiah says, "I am doing a great work, so that I cannot come down. . . ." How many people try to get you to come down from your work in the church every week? Tell them, "I am doing a great work, and I can't come down!"

Many came to Nehemiah. Even so-called friends tried to convince him that he was not doing what he was supposed to be doing. "Don't rebuild that wall. Come on down and let's talk about it. You don't know what you're doing." Just like Nehemiah did, do not listen! We are building a wall; we are building a place of safety, a haven, a place of rest, a place of prayer for you and your family.

If everybody is in their place, doing what they are supposed to be doing for the Kingdom of God, it will be a secure place, and a wall will get built. Every brick, every piece of mortar, everything that must happen to make a wall go up will happen, and you will see it. Most buildings will not be big enough to contain the people. You will have to have another building; you will have to have another location. It will take more people finding their place in the Ministry of Helps.

Sometimes you cannot take another step forward until you get the commitment from the people to walk there with you.

Pastors cannot ask God to send them souls if they do not have altar workers to work with the people to lead them to the Lord or they do not have enough nursery workers to take on the twenty more babies they are going to get. They will not get the growth they are praying for until you are in your place, and that is every particular individual who is supposed to be doing what they are doing for God.

This is not a time to draw back; it is a time to rejoice and get excited!

5

Faithfulness in Serving

Proverbs 28:20 says, *"A faithful man shall abound with blessings. . . ."* Gill's Commentary says, "A **man of faithfulness.** A very faithful man, that is truly so; that is so in a moral sense; true to his work, makes good his promises, fulfills his contracts, abides by the obligations he lays himself under; is faithful in every trust reposed in him, be it greater or lesser matters, in every station in which it is, and throughout the whole course of his life."

God wants to bless your life. He is showing you a way that you can get blessed, even far above and more abundantly!

It was because of my faithfulness that blessings came. I did not confess for some of the things that God gave me, but because of my faithfulness I received those blessings. God just blessed me with them. One person came up to me and said, "I've been watching you and you have been faithful, and so God wants me to bless you."

Where is the blessing line? It is the faithful line. Be the part that God has called you to be! It is the individual supplying what God called them to supply, doing it with the right attitude and the right heart, which is a servant's heart, rendering service unto people. That is what God wants you to do. Every member has been selected; therefore, you are important. Every member of this Body is especially important. You are a particular part, and the pastor and staff are praying for people to stand up and be counted. They are praying for people to be in the place and position where they are supposed to be, serving God with him.

Leadership is praying for more musicians. Usually they do not have enough musicians. The local church never has enough singers, nursery workers, or parking lot attendants. We want no one individual burned out because they are working for God.

Nehemiah, concerning the wall he was rebuilding, knew that the work was important, and he could not leave it. I have had people try to get me to do things that I was not supposed to do because they wanted me to do something with them. That would have taken me away from the work I was doing. They were not malicious in their heart; they were just people.

I had this challenge one time. A Christian organization always had a golf tournament every year at the same time as a convention on Sunday morning which would keep those involved from church. About four or five years went by, and then this Christian organization said, "You know, we're not getting a good response." So, they changed it from Sunday to Saturday, and the next time they could not hold all the participants who wanted to support it.

Do not get caught up and let things pull you away from what God is calling

Faithfulness in Serving

you to do in your local church. God thinks that standing at that back door is just as precious as standing on the platform. God believes that standing in the parking lot, or opening someone's car door is just as precious as standing behind a pulpit. We must be committed, and we will be if we understand that our work is important.

WHAT YOU ARE DOING IS IMPORTANT!

Do you understand that what you are doing is important? I have shared Scripture with you to show you that there is a calling, a distinct calling of God for the Ministry of Helps. I shared with you, and you have seen the challenges and difference in people's lives that it makes.

Just think how important it was when an usher moved with an anointing and caught someone who fell under the power of God, or an altar worker shares the gospel with someone, and they got saved. Everyone in their place.

How precious and how much of a treasure that God sees in the Ministry of Helps. It is like a chest full of jewels to Him. He looks down and sees the Ministry of Helps and sees it working and operating, every member in their place, doing what they are supposed to be doing for Him. The reward for it is so incredible.

I am so excited that God allowed me for all the years to be involved with the Ministry of Helps. I do not have to stop just because I am ministering from a pulpit. I can still serve and have a servant's heart in everything that I do. I am not too good to serve any one of you. You are not too good to serve me.

Faithfulness in Serving

We do not put accountability on your status in life. Remember when I shared that with you in the beginning? It is not status. It is not because I dress nicer, wear nicer clothes, or drive a different car. There is no status in that. All those things are rewards and blessings. I drive what I drive. I dress the way I dress because the blessings of God are overtaking me because of my faithfulness to Him. I will serve where He asks me to serve with a heart that is willing to do what He has called me to do. Amen!

Proverbs 28:19 AMP says, *"He who cultivates his land will have plenty of bread, but he who follows worthless people and frivolous pursuits will have plenty of poverty."*

You say, "What does that have to do with the Ministry of Helps?" Well, if you are in a local church, is that your land? Are you cultivating and working in your land? You are not working over in the church's land across town. You are working in your home church! You are called here to cultivate your land. Solomon says, "If you cultivate your land, you will have plenty of bread."

Let me paraphrase it for you. "He who works his ground will have abundant food, but the man who chases, runs here and there, and never sticks to anything, any job, any place, any church, will have his fill of poverty." In other words, God expects you to be committed to where you are at—your church. He expects you to be working and involved in it, doing what you are supposed to be doing. He wants you to help your church accomplish its vision, so we can see Him come and manifest His glory.

Faithfulness in Serving

We must know that everyone of us has a place to minister in the Body. It is an important place, and it is a good work. I believe what I am doing is a good work. I have believed it since the day I got saved. I did that in 1974. Right before Thanksgiving, I attended a Charles and Francis Hunter meeting. God divinely and supernaturally healed me, saved me, and delivered me from drugs and alcohol all in one night. My wife was saved before me, and the Lord told her to pray that something good would happen to me to draw me to God.

It was during the time that people were saying to pray for bad things to happen to someone to bring them to God. But Kathy had a knowing on the inside of her that that was not true. I had a bad car wreck and lived by the grace of God. I had rods and staples in one of my legs. I had a two inch buildup with one of my shoes and walked with a cane. The doctor told me I would be that way the rest of my life, and I would not be able to bend my knee. I had already had plenty of bad things that happened to me, but God's goodness came and healed me and delivered me, I got saved that night! I have been in the Ministry of Helps since that day.

Basically I started working in the Ministry of Helps, and I did not even know what it was. I started going to the church, sweeping and mowing the lawn. I just wanted to do something for the Lord. I never heard about Helps until 1976, a few years later when I moved to Tulsa. That is when I first heard the teaching on the Ministry of Helps. I did not know what I was doing.

Faithfulness in Serving

And today, a lot of people do not know what they're doing. They want to do something, but they do not know why. They want to work. They want to help. They will come and sweep and vacuum the sanctuary. They would come and help in many different areas until they knew specifically what God was telling them to do on a regular basis.

If you are not working and doing something in church, just come and show up and do anything that your hands find to do because God will prosper it. God will prosper you getting involved. When the church says, "We are going to have a cleaning day," and four people show up that are the regular cleaning people, that is not going to benefit you. They are going to get blessed, and if you show up, you will be blessed also.

In the beginning I did not know what I was doing. I did not know that when I was going and straightening up chairs because it looked untidy to me that I was flowing in the Ministry of Helps. I enjoyed doing it.

I found a commentary of 1 Corinthians 12:28. In referring to the word "Helps," it used the word "revelation," which inferred that Helps was a supernatural perception from God to accomplish something as a member in the Body of Christ. I was doing something that God was instilling in my heart that would last a lifetime. The blessings began to follow me!

Stay Faithful to the Vision

I had men who offered me jobs because they saw I was a faithful man. I was faithful to the organization to which God had called me. One time I was offered

Faithfulness in Serving

a position by another company during the time of being faithful to the company to which God called me. It would have taken me away from the vision to which I was called.

They offered me $200,000 a year salary, a $1,000,000 bonus, and the company at the end of five years. Kathy and I talked and prayed. The offer sounded wonderful. The salary was way more than I made, and I would have been running the company. We did not mind moving to another state, but as Kathy and I prayed some more, we knew it was not right.

We met back with him and said "No!" He said, "Okay, what if I pay you $100,000 a year, pay all your expenses to fly up here to my company two days a month? But you cannot work with any other company, and that is all you must do. Just consult with me for two days a month, and I'll pay all your expenses here and back and give you $100,000 a year." But we knew it was still "No." The enticement to move you from your place can come in different forms, and it will always look good. But do not come off your wall!

Proverbs 20:6 says, *"Most men will proclaim every one his own goodness: but a faithful man who can find?"*

Proverbs 25:13 says, *"As the cold of snow in the time of harvest, so is a faithful messenger to them that send him: for he refresheth the soul of his masters."*

I had an earthly master, and I have a heavenly Master. I was serving both the way that I believe I was supposed to be serving them. I was doing what I was supposed to be doing until God told me different. Sometimes I found myself doing things that were not specifically a call. When my earthly master needed his car parked, that's not part of my calling to the company, but it's part of my servant's heart. Big difference when you find that out! Success will follow you all the days of your life if you have that attitude in your heart. Amen!

Let me finish with a couple of Scriptures here.

First Timothy 4:14 says, *"Neglect not the gift that is in thee, which was given thee by prophecy, with the laying on of the hands of the presbytery."*

Most of you have had words of prophecy given to you, or someone laid hands on you, or someone confirmed something God had spoken in your heart. Are you doing it? Do what you are supposed to do and get blessed! I'm not here to condemn you. I'm here to help you get blessed. I'm here to tell you that it is very important that you understand that if you do what you know you're supposed to be doing from your heart, you are going to get blessed. God is going to perform His Word! He is going to bless you!

Second Timothy 1:6 says, *"Wherefore I put thee in remembrance that thou stir up the gift of God, which is in thee by the putting on of my hands."*

Some of you have already been in prayer lines where hands were laid on you. Some of you do not know what you are supposed be doing for God. There is one simple way to find out. Ask God!

Then share with your pastor or leaders your desire to serve. If you have anything

Faithfulness in Serving

in your heart, share that with them, then trust them. The pastor was given the responsibility to lead the people he was given by God. Serve with all your heart, mind, and strength. Do not let people talk you out of it. Do not let them tell you it is not a good work! It is a great work! It magnifies, glorifies, and honors God just as much as someone preaching from the pulpit in great crusades. It magnifies God just as much when obeying Him in the Ministry of Helps as someone ministering in their healing crusades and prayer seminars. It honors God just as much! Amen!

I trust something is stirring in your heart! Saying "yes" to the Lord brings peace. As you have read this book, my prayer is that it will stir you to get involved or want to do more. Saying "yes" to the Lord in serving in your local church will bring one of the greatest things in your life—peace. I love having peace in my life. I love knowing that God's on the throne, and peace is ruling and reigning in my heart.

Spiritual Hunger

The Ministry of Helps is found among spiritually hungry people who are coming in this move. They are gentle and loving individuals who give love and who may have served in the local church before with all their hearts. They are usually the willing servants, the best givers, and the most faithful to the church. They understand how to honor the pastor and his appointed leaders. Spiritual hunger in the lives of these people will force a search for food that has been missing.

We must give these people true spiritual substance, not a story about Him; true worship, not merely songs. They need His manifested presence, not an intellectual discussion about His presence. They need to experience Him and Him alone. They need to be challenged and drawn to Him, encouraged, and released into His presence.

These people are in the most unlikely places and are the most common, but you will recognize the fire in their eyes, the glory in their smile, the hope in their conversation, and the love in their service.

Some of those who are coming may be on the sidelines and just do not know how to get back into the church. The leaders must be willing to give of themselves and be the right part to get them back into the place of their calling to serve. We must develop a place of refreshing, restoration, and renewal for them so we again can hear their song, even when they are not singing, and see the light in their eyes even in the dark.

6

Joy and Peace in Serving

Serving is an expression of who we are, an expression of the nature we share with God. I have come to understand that my greatest joy comes from the act of serving and the approval of my heavenly Father!

All work is sacred when the worker is in right relationship with God. Then the joy of work is its own reward.

As a young man, I looked for work that would satisfy me. I accepted as many as twenty different jobs over about a five-year period after returning from Vietnam. Nothing could bring the joy of working. It was never about the people, but the work being performed. I have talked to many people in the work force today who are on a job which seems just to be an end to the means, boring and lifeless. I think sometimes this attitude has crept into the church, and many of those working is just that—working. They have not gained the understanding of the call, so they are just working.

Jesus has an amazing ability to match the individual member with the job, the person with the position. In fact, two of the ways to determine if you are in the right place of serving is how well your yoke fits, and is your serving refreshing and not a burden.

Matthew 11:29 states, *"Take my yoke upon you, and learn of me. . . ."*

You say, "What is a yoke?" Realizing that a lot of those coming to the church today may not have heard this word, I will define it for you. Jesus said that His yoke was easy and His burden light, which is referring to His ways of doing things after repentance. A yoke is a type of harness which connects two animals together for the purpose of plowing, pulling a wagon, etc. This reference is to indicate that when you are connected with Jesus and understand that His ways are now your ways, it will be easy and not burdensome. When He says He is a servant, we now need to yoke ourselves (connect) with Him, and find our place to serve in the Body as members in particular.

Another way of saying this is, if the member is joined to serve, it will be with joy and peace as a member in particular, not tied together serving in a wrong place of ministry in the church. The Ministry of Helps must never be a form of bondage. Find a yoke (your place of connection to the call) that fits and wear it! Make sure your attitude is right, and make sure you have a servant's heart!

WHEN HURT AND FAILURE SEEM TO HAPPEN

Love does not see the past, only the present and what is available for you in the future. Many Christians have found themselves in the place in the Ministry of Helps where wrong decisions or others' view of them has put them in the place of regret or wanting to quit and live on the sidelines of life. I always say, "I refuse to allow anyone else to frame my world, because they will always frame it too small."

When hurt and failure seem to happen, our world shrinks and becomes an introverted view of what is going on around us. This is when despair and despondency creep in and tell us it is no use to try to serve because no one sees our true value or potential.

Let's look at something I received one morning during prayer. Three words came to me:

DEPRESSION, DESPONDENT, DESPAIR

Depression means low in spirit, dejected, hollow, suffering because of social and economical hardship, inability to concentrate, feeling rejected. This can cause you to take on the characteristic of

The Heart of Helps

self-reliant, which means fulfillment of one's self or one's own potential.

Despondent means disheartened because of loss of hope which leads to loss of courage and confidence. Rejection sets in and leads to pride, which means a sense of one's own self-value and dignity or self-satisfaction from one's own work, achievements, possessions, an overly high opinion of one's self.

Despair means that which is reduced in rank or esteem, to be overcome by a sense of futility or defeat, utter lack of hope or something destroying all hope.

These three in succession will lead you to **deception,** which means: to cause to believe in what is not true, misled, to be foiled, hoodwinked, taken in, or a cause to accept the false. I know this part can be overwhelming but just pause here and reread it several times before going on.

This is when the deceiver comes and brings the false accusation or lies, which cause you to see what he wants, and defeat comes. Defeat comes only if you accept his lies and agree with him. Therefore many of those members in particular are setting on the sidelines of life causing the local churches to be weak as a Body.

Pastor Paul Brady of Living Rivers Millennial Church in Tulsa made a statement one time about the Body of Christ that I liked. He said, *"Where do I fit? But you will never find it while you sit! But in this place be mobilized, and you will see it was a supernatural fit."*

Jude 2 MSG says, *"Relax, everything's going to be all right; rest, everything's coming together; open your hearts, love is on the way!"*

My wonderful wife, Kathy, has been like a rose blooming and as each petal unfolds, it shows an expression of love. Many times I wanted to just give up because of the outcome of decisions either I made or others made. But as I humbled myself and saw it from the Father's eyes, I would see another petal from my wife's expression of love reaching out to the situation and responding as God does. She showed love to the situation and the results always gave way to the beauty of forgiveness.

Then I would ask myself what I needed to do to correct myself to move forward with the call of God in my life, not what I thought needed to be done in a part of the ministry where I was unable to change the outcome.

A statement from Dr. Buddy Harrison, who was a very influential person in my

Joy and Peace in Serving

life, comes to mind: "You can only change the outcome of a situation when you are in the place to make the decision to bring about that change." It is just as important to learn what you cannot do as what you can do. When you are working in a place that does not fit you, it becomes heavy because your investment of serving has become expenditure. Do you enjoy doing what you do?

Most people, left to their own intuition, will gravitate to their areas of giftedness. Many people spend a lifetime not following their heart to serve, and they never know the joy of serving which brings fulfillment. We are co-laborers with God!

7

SEEING THE GRAND SCHEME WHILE SERVING

I want to share a story with you. The architect of St. Paul's Cathedral was admiring the work of the gentleman mixing cement for the bricklayers, and he stopped to ask him his job. He answered, "Sir, can't you see, I am building a great Cathedral!"

As the Ministry of Helps, we must see the big picture of what we are helping to build.

When we are serving, we need to look beyond the job and see the grand scheme, and claim it as our own.

Ephesians 4:11-13 TPT states:

And he has appointed some with grace to be apostles, and some with grace to be prophets, and some with grace to be evangelists, and some with grace to be pastors, and some with grace to be teachers.

And their calling is to nurture and prepare all the holy believers to do their own works of ministry, and as they do this they will enlarge and build up the body of Christ.

These grace ministries will <u>function</u> until we all attain oneness in *the faith, until we all experience the fullness of what it means to know the Son of God, and finally we become one perfect man with the full dimensions of spiritual maturity and fully developed in the abundance of Christ.*

Pastors Are Looking for Men and Women

Acts 6:2-3 TPT says:

"The twelve apostles called a meeting of all the believers and told them, 'It is not advantageous for us to be pulled away from the word of God to wait on tables.

"'We want you to carefully select from among yourselves seven godly men. Make sure they are honorable, full of the Holy Spirit and wisdom, and we will give them the responsibility of this crucial ministry of serving.'"

Pastors are looking for men and women who will take their place in the crucial Ministry of Helps, serving in the local church to see an abundant harvest for Christ!

With no limitations, no hesitations, and no reservations in any shape or form, they will move in a mighty way because they know their place. They will be trained in skilled servanthood, moving with rhythm and at ease with other members jointly fit together. They will be efficient and graceful in response to God's plan. They are fully developed within and without. They will stay focused, pray, and obey the assignment, whatever it is. They are not looking for a title, but will pour out what is in them, and it will always be what is needed. God will not ask them to do something based on limitations, but on His limitlessness working in them.

Seeing the Grand Scheme While Serving

Always be led by the Spirit, and you will have no regrets. If everyone is in their place and yielded to the Spirit of God, the Spirit will kindle the fire; and people will come from far and wide to see God's love manifested.

I am going to close with this statement again from Pastor Paul Brady. He said, "Where do I fit? But you will never find it while you sit! But in this place be mobilized, and you will see it was a supernatural fit."

ABOUT THE AUTHOR

Author Tom Rutherford was ordained in 1983.

He has served in the Ministry of Helps for over forty years.

One of the ministries where he served for twenty-three years had three facets to it: a church, a ministers' organization, and a Christian publishing company. Tom traveled with this minister to the churches and pastors where he had relationships. This taught Tom a lot about the government of the local church and the needs and desires of the pastors and their congregations.

In the publishing industry, Tom was brought before many ministers and heard and saw the things that ministers are confronted with in their ministries and their personal lives. With this experience and training, God has equipped him for such a time as this.

Tom has been empowered to unlock and break open what is needed to bring the Ministry of Helps alive in churches, and align many in the Body of Christ to God's plans and purposes for their lives. The focus is to activate and show how each member in the Body of Christ is equipped to help the Ministry Gifts fulfill the vision God has given them. The goal is to train and mobilize strong, Word-based, and Spirit-led men and women who will be proficient in the operations of the Spirit of God and have the heart for their part.

He wants everyone in the Body of Christ to be a visible, realistic standard of the servanthood in the local church by doing what they are supposed be doing for God!

To contact:

Tom Rutherford
P. O. Box 120081
Melbourne, Florida 32912 U.S.A.
tomrutherford14@yahoo.com